Echlin Surname

Ireland: 1600s to 1900s

From Ireland Church Records of Baptism, Marriage and Death

Comprised of Roman Catholic and Church of Ireland Records

From Counties Carlow, Cork, Kerry and Dublin City

Compiled by **Donovan Hurst**

May 7, 2013

ISBN: 1939958180
ISBN-13: 978-1-939958-18-1

Dedication

This work is dedicated to all of those that came before us and shaped our lives to make us the people that we are today.

Table of Contents

Introduction

This is a compilation of individuals who have the surname of Echlin that lived in the country of Ireland from the 1600s to the 1900s. I have placed each entry into one of four categories: Families, Individual Births/Baptisms, Individual Burials, and Individual Marriages. If a marriage entry primarily concerns an Individual Echlin whom is female, then I have placed that entry under the category of Individual Marriages. If a marriage entry primarily concerns an Individual Echlin whom is male, then I have placed that entry under the category of Families. Images of many of these listings are available at http://churchrecords.irishgenealogy.ie/churchrecords/.

To help guide the reader of this work, the format of this book is as follows:

- Main Family Entry (Husband and Wife) (Father and Mother)

    o Child of Main Family Entry, including Spouse(s) when available

        ▪ Grandchild of Main Family Entry, including Spouse(s) when available

            • Great-Grandchild of Main Family Entry, including Spouse(s) when available

(**Bolded Text**) following any entry includes any additional information such as Residence(s), Occupation(s), Signature(s), etc. when available.

Hurst

Some of the fonts used in this work symbolizes Celtic writing. The traditional letters, numbers, and punctuation marks and their Celtic counterparts are as follows:

Traditional Letters (Uppercase & Lowercase)

A a B b C c D d E f G g H h I i J j K k L l M m N n O o P p Q q R r S s T t U u V v W w X x Y y Z z

Celtic Letters (Uppercase & Lowercase)

A a B b C c D ð E e F ꝼ G g H h I í J j K k L l M m

N n O o P p Q q R r S s T t U u V v W w X x Y y Z z

Traditional Numbers

1 2 3 4 5 6 7 8 9 10

Celtic Numbers

1 2 3 4 5 6 7 8 9 10

Traditional Punctuation

. , : ' " & - ( )

Celtic Punctuation

. , : ' " & - ( )

Parish Churches

Carlow (Church of Ireland)

Carlow Parish, Tullow Parish, and Urglin Parish.

Dublin (Church of Ireland)

Bethseda Chapel Parish, Grangegorman Parish, North Strand Parish, Rathmines Parish, Rotunda Chapel Parish, St. Audoen Parish, St. Bride Parish, St. Catherine Parish, St. George Parish, St. James Parish, St. John Parish, St. Luke Parish, St. Mark Parish, St. Mary Parish, St. Michan Parish, St. Nicholas Without Parish, St. Paul Parish, St. Peter Parish, St. Thomas Parish, and St. Werburgh Parish.

Dublin (Roman Catholic or RC)

Rathmines Parish, SS. Michael & John Parish, St. Andrew Parish, St. Catherine Parish, St. James Parish, St. Lawrence Parish, St. Mary, Pro Cathedral Parish, St. Michan Parish, and St. Nicholas Parish.

Families

- Abraham Echlin & Unknown

  - Thomas Echlin – bapt. 15 Dec 1661 (Baptism, **St. John Parish**)

- Anthony Echlin & Anne Savage

  - Catherine Echlin – bapt. 28 Jul 1783 (Baptism, **St. Michan Parish (RC)**)

  - Catherine Echlin – bapt. 21 Apr 1789 (Baptism, **St. James Parish (RC)**)

- Anthony Echlin & Unknown

  - William Echlin – bapt. 1 May 1643 (Baptism, **St. John Parish**)

- Charles Echlin & Anne Graham – 1 Jan 1795 (Marriage, **St. Peter Parish**)

- Charles Echlin & Elizabeth Echlin

  - George Woods Echlin – b. 29 Sep 1846, bapt. 8 Nov 1846 (Baptism, **St. Mary Parish**)

Charles Echlin (father):

Residence - 43 Mary Street - November 8, 1846

Occupation - Gentleman - November 8, 1846

- Charles Echlin & Elizabeth Echlin

  - Margaret Echlin – b. 10 Feb 1850, bapt. 19 May 1850 (Baptism, **Rathmines Parish**)

Charles Echlin (father):

Residence - Homeville, Rathmines Road - May 19, 1850

Occupation - Clerk in the Board of Works - May 19, 1850

Hurst

- Charles Echlin & Susanna Boyce – 21 Feb 1808 (Marriage, **St. Peter Parish**)

  - Robert Henry Echlin – b. 1814, bapt. 21 Aug 1814 (Baptism, **St. James Parish**)

- Charles John Cavendish Echlin & Margaret Helena Echlin

  - Maude Alicia Echlin – b. 7 Oct 1888, bapt. 2 Dec 1888 (Baptism, **North Strand Parish**)

  - Florence Edith Echlin – b. 7 Jan 1890, bapt. 2 Feb 1890 (Baptism, **North Strand Parish**)

  - Lucy Margaret Echlin – b. 25 Feb 1891, bapt. 7 May 1891 (Baptism, **North Strand Parish**)

  - Charles John Cavendish Echlin – b. 23 Jan 1895, bapt. 10 Mar 1895 (Baptism, **North Strand Parish**)

Charles John Cavendish Echlin (father):

Residence - 38 Upper Rutland Street - December 2, 1888

8 Summerhill Parade - February 2, 1890

3 Windsor Avenue - May 7, 1891

49 Upper Rutland Street - March 10, 1895

Occupation - Clerk - December 2, 1888

February 2, 1890

March 10, 1895

Law Clerk - May 7, 1891

- Christian Echlin & Mary Echlin

  - William Echlin – bur. 29 Jun 1692 (Burial, **St. Michan Parish**)

Christian Echlin (father):

Occupation - Sugar Baker - June 29, 1692

Echlin Surname Ireland: 1600s to 1900s

- Christopher Echlin & Anne Echlin

    o Christopher Echlin – bapt. 10 Apr 1726 (Baptism, **Urglin Parish**), bur. 9 Oct 1728 (Burial, **Urglin Parish**)

Christopher Echlin (son):

Residence - Burton Hall, Urglin Parish - before October 9, 1728

- Christopher Echlin & Anne Elizabeth Echlin

    o Christopher Echlin – bapt. 21 Nov 1700 (Baptism, **St. Mary Parish**)

    o William Echlin – bapt. 11 Apr 1702 (Baptism, **St. Mary Parish**)

    o Elizabeth Echlin – b. 26 Jul 1703, bapt. 1 Aug 1703(Baptism, **St. Mary Parish**), bur. 11 Nov 1703 (Burial, **St. Mary Parish**)

    o Jane Echlin – b. 29 Jan 1705, bapt. 2 Feb 1705 (Baptism, **St. Mary Parish**)

    o John Echlin – b. 30 Mar 1706, bapt. 2 Apr 1706 (Baptism, **St. Mary Parish**), bur. 18 Jun 1707 (Burial, **St. Mary Parish**)

    o Charles Echlin – b. 20 Mar 1708, bapt. 24 Mar 1708 (Baptism, **St. Mary Parish**)

    o Elizabeth Echlin – b. 6 Aug 1710, bapt. 10 Aug 1710 (Baptism, **St. Mary Parish**)

Christopher Echlin (father):

Occupation - Coach Man - November 21, 1700

April 11, 1702

August 1, 1703

November 11, 1703

February 2, 1705

Hurst

April 2, 1706

June 18, 1707

March 24, 1708

August 10, 1710

- Christopher Echlin & Esther Nearman (N e a r m a n) – 27 Feb 1767 (Marriage, **St. Catherine Parish**)

- Edward Echlin & Catherine Echlin

  o Margaret Charles Echlin – bapt. 16 Nov 1807 (Baptism, **St. Paul Parish**)

- Edward Echlin & Elizabeth Byrne (B y r n e)

  o Mary Margaret Echlin – b. 1886, bapt. 1886 (Baptism, **St. Andrew Parish (RC)**)

Edward Echlin (father):

Residence - 2 Fleet Street - 1886

- Edward Echlin & Mary Ballantyne – 11 Feb 1843 (Marriage, **St. George Parish**)

Signatures:

Edward Echlin (husband):

Residence - Belfast, Co. Antrim - February 11, 1843

Hutton's Lane, St. George Parish - February 11, 1843

Echlín Surname Ireland: 1600s to 1900s

Mary Ballantyne (wife):

Residence - Belfast, Co. Antrim - February 11, 1843

Hutton's Lane, St. George Parish - February 11, 1843

Wedding Witnesses:

John Kennedy, Margaret McCartney, & James Edmiston

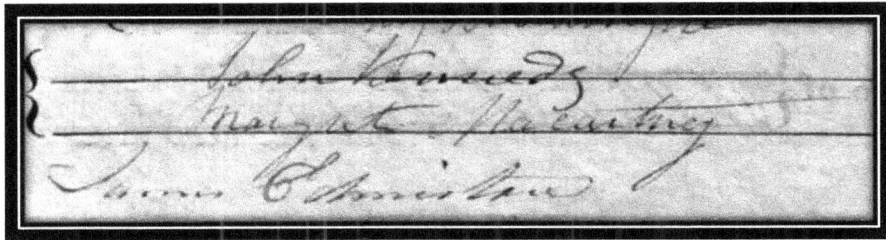

Signatures:

- Edward Moore Echlin, b. 1783, bur. 8 Mar 1836 (Burial, **St. Mary Parish**) & Catherine Echlin

  o John Echlin – b. 1813, bapt. 12 Feb 1813 (Baptism, **St. Catherine Parish**)

  o Maria Echlin – b. 1815, bapt. 22 Feb 1815 (Baptism, **St. Catherine Parish**)

  o Edward Echlin – b. 20 Jun 1817, bapt. 21 Jun 1817 (Baptism, **St. Catherine Parish**)

  o Catherine Echlin – b. 26 May 1819, bapt. 28 May 1819 (Baptism, **St. Catherine Parish**)

  o William Echlin – b. 20 Jun 1821, bapt. 5 Jul 1821 (Baptism, **St. Catherine Parish**)

  o Elizabeth Echlin – b. 3 May 1824, bapt. 12 May 1824 (Baptism, **St. Catherine Parish**)

  o William Frederick Echlin – b. 24 Jun 1827, bapt. 24 Jun 1827 (Baptism, **St. Catherine Parish**)

Edward Moore Echlin (father):

Residence - Crane Street - June 21, 1817

May 28, 1819

May 12, 1824

Hurst

June 24, 1827

before March 8, 1836

Age at Death - 53 years

- Edward Moore Echlin & Ellen Echlin

  o Edward Moore Echlin – b. 28 Jul 1849, bapt. 9 Sep 1849 (Baptism, **St. Werburgh Parish**)

  o Emily Jane Echlin – b. 7 Feb 1851, bapt. 24 Aug 1851 (Baptism, **St. Werburgh Parish**)

  o Eleanor Echlin – b. 27 Jul 1853, bapt. 17 Aug 1853 (Baptism, **St. George Parish**)

Edward Moore Echlin (father):

Residence - 25 Werburgh Street - September 9, 1849

39 Castle Street - August 24, 1851

28 Upper Dorset Street - August 17, 1853

Occupation - House Painter - September 9, 1849

August 24, 1851

August 17, 1853

- Edward Moore Echlin & Unknown

  o Edward Moore Echlin & Anne Power Hynes – 9 Jun 1877 (Marriage, **St. Mark Parish**)

Signatures:

Echlin Surname Ireland: 1600s to 1900s

- Eva Adelaide Echlin – b. 23 Sep 1878, bapt. 28 Sep 1878 (Baptism, **St. Mark Parish**)

- Eleanor Evelyn Echlin – b. 23 Aug 1879, bapt. 27 May 1880 (Baptism, **St. Mary, Pro Cathedral Parish (RC)**), bapt. 2 Jul 1882 (Baptism, **Bethseda Chapel Parish**)

- Cecil Moore Echlin – b. 16 May 1882, bapt. 28 Jun 1882 (Baptism, **St. Mary, Pro Cathedral Parish (RC)**), bapt. 2 Jul 1882 (Baptism, **Bethseda Chapel Parish**)

- Thomas Power Echlin – b. 29 Sep 1884, bapt. 25 Sep 1891 (Baptism, **Grangegorman Parish**)

- Anne Echlin – b. 30 Dec 1886, bapt. 25 Sep 1891 (Baptism, **Grangegorman Parish**)

- Edward Joseph Echlin – b. 17 Feb 1889, bapt. 25 Sep 1891 (Baptism, **Grangegorman Parish**)

- Kathleen Echlin – b. 28 Feb 1892, bapt. 4 Sep 1892 (Baptism, **Grangegorman Parish**)

- Robert Echlin – b. March 1892, bur. 30 Aug 1892 (Burial, **St. George Parish**)

Robert Echlin (son):

Residence - **21 St. Ignatius Road** - before **August 30, 1892**

Age at Death - **6 months**

Edward Moore Echlin (son):

Residence - **161 Townsend Street** - June 9, **1877**

162 Townsend Street - September 28, **1878**

40 Great Britain Street - May 27, **1880**

June 28, **1882**

79 Albert Road, Sandy Cove - July 2, **1882**

21 St. Ignatius Road - September 25, **1891**

September 4, **1892**

Hurst

Occupation - Commercial Clerk - June 9, 1877

Commercial Traveller - September 28, 1878

July 2, 1882

September 25, 1891

September 4, 1892

Anne Power Hynes, daughter of Patrick Power (daughter-in-law):

Residence - 161 Townsend Street - June 9, 1877

Relationship Status at Marriage - widow

Patrick Power (father):

Occupation - Railway Clerk

Edward Moore Echlin (father):

Occupation - Gentleman

Wedding Witnesses:

William McCord & Martha Longhran

Signatures:

Echlin Surname Ireland: 1600s to 1900s

- Ferdinand Echlin & Unknown

  o John Echlin & Harriet Jane Kennedy, b. 1850 – 5 May 1869 (Marriage, **St. Mark Parish**)

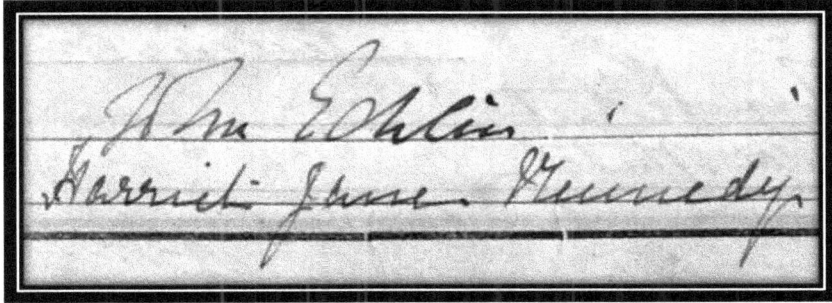

Signatures:

- Leticia Mary Echlin – b. 5 May 1870, bapt. 25 May 1870 (Baptism, **St. Mary Parish**)

- Evelyn Marion Echlin – b. 10 Nov 1871, bapt. 6 Dec 1871 (Baptism, **St. Mary Parish**)

- Martha Emily Echlin – b. 4 Mar 1879, bapt. 12 Mar 1879 (Baptism, **St. George Parish**)

- Charlotte Mary Echlin – b. 20 Nov 1881, bapt. 14 Dec 1881 (Baptism, **St. George Parish**)

- John Frederick Echlin – b. 18 Sep 1890, bapt. 15 Oct 1890 (Baptism, **St. George Parish**)

- Richard Brabason Moore Echlin – b. 3 Oct 1894, bapt. 4 Nov 1894 (Baptism, **St. Mary Parish**)

- [Hard to Read] inleen Alexandria Echlin – b. Unclear, bapt. Unclear (Baptism, **St. Thomas Parish**)

[Hard to Read] **inleen Alexandria Echlin (daughter):**

Remarks about Birth - The church register entry was burned in a fire and the

information containing her first name, birth date, and

baptism date is missing.

Hurst

John Echlin (son):

Residence - 50 Townsend Street - May 5, 1869

74 Upper Dominick Street - May 25, 1870

59 Upper Dominick Street - December 6, 1871

Royal Canal, Blackquiere Bridge - March 12, 1879

Phibsborough - December 14, 1881

11 Whitworth Place - October 15, 1890

22 Palmerston Place - November 4, 1894

100 Amiens Street - Unclear

Occupation - Servant - May 5, 1869

Mercantile Clerk - May 25, 1870

Clerk, M. G. W. R. Co. - December 6, 1871

Station Master - March 12, 1879

Clerk - December 14, 1881

October 15, 1890

November 4, 1894

Unclear

Harriet Jane Kennedy, daughter of George Kennedy (daughter-in-law):

Residence - 50 Townsend Street - May 5, 1869

Age at Marriage - 19 years

Echlin Surname Ireland: 1600s to 1900s

George Kennedy (father):

Occupation - Constable

Ferdinand Echlin (father):

Occupation - Gentleman

Wedding Witnesses:

George Fermen & Catherine Delaney

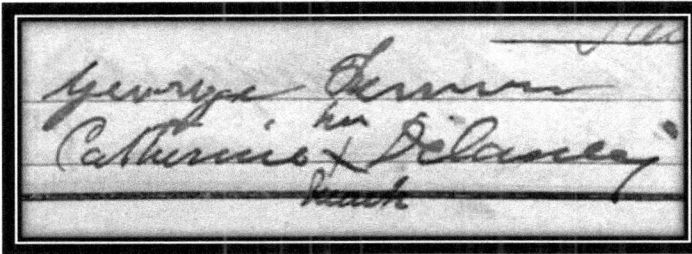

Signatures:

- Francis Hamilton Echlin & Anne Elizabeth Echlin

    o Daniel Moore Echlin – bapt. 21 Dec 1806 (Baptism, **St. Mary Parish**)

    o Michael Echlin – bapt. 21 Apr 1808 (Baptism, **St. Mary Parish**)

    o Alice Echlin – bapt. 5 Oct 1809, bapt. 5 Nov 1809 (Baptism, **St. Mary Parish**)

    o Francis Hamilton Echlin – bapt. 12 May 1811 (Baptism, **St. Mary Parish**)

- Francis Echlin & Mary Fleming

    o Bridget Echlin – bapt. 20 Nov 1743 (Baptism, **St. Catherine Parish (RC)**)

    o William Echlin – bapt. 26 Apr 1747 (Baptism, **St. Catherine Parish (RC)**)

- George Echlin & Anne Jane O'Brien – 26 Jun 1831 (Marriage, **St. Mary Parish**)

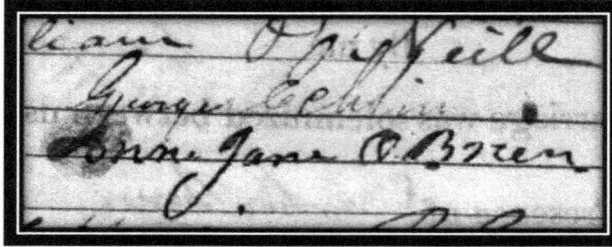

Signatures:

George Echlin (husband):

Residence - St. Mary Parish - June 26, 1831

Anne Jane O'Brien (wife):

Residence - St. Mary Parish - June 26, 1831

James McClay & J. L .Hosie

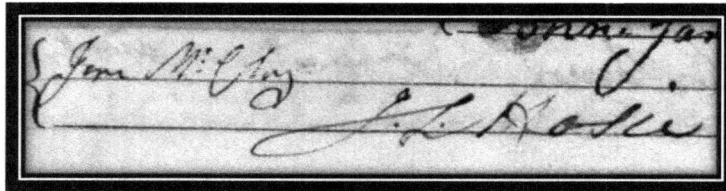

Signatures:

- George Echlin & Bridget Byrne (B y r n e)
  - Elizabeth Echlin – bapt. 12 Dec 1779 (Baptism, **St. Catherine Parish** (RC))
  - James Echlin – bapt. 12 Dec 1779 (Baptism, **St. Catherine Parish** (RC))
  - Thomas Echlin – bapt. 19 Feb 1782 (Baptism, **St. Catherine Parish** (RC))
- George Echlin & Elizabeth Unknown
  - George Echlin – bapt. 1826 (Baptism, **St. Andrew Parish** (RC))

Echlín Surname Ireland: 1600s to 1900s

- George Echlin & Esther Leech – 22 Oct 1838 (Marriage, **St. Andrew Parish (RC)**)

  - Thomas Echlin – bapt. 1840 (Baptism, **St. Andrew Parish (RC)**)

  - Catherine Echlin – bapt. 1844 (Baptism, **St. Andrew Parish (RC)**)

Wedding Witnesses:

Michael Gormley & Anne Purcell

- George Echlin & Margaret Flaherty

  - Roseanne Echlin – b. 12 Nov 1877, bapt. 26 Nov 1877 (Baptism, **St. Michan Parish (RC)**)

  - Charles John Echlin – b. 26 Jan 1881, bapt. 4 Feb 1881 (Baptism, **St. Mary, Pro Cathedral Parish (RC)**)

  - Margaret Anne Echlin – b. 10 Sep 1882, bapt. 11 Sep 1882 (Baptism, **St. Michan Parish (RC)**)

  - Catherine Echlin – b. 23 Feb 1887, bapt. 2 Mar 1887 (Baptism, **St. Michan Parish (RC)**)

George Echlin (father):

Residence - 2 Henrietta Lane - November 26, 1877

9 Bolton Street - February 4, 1881

7 Lurgan Street - September 11, 1882

3 Lisburn Street - March 2, 1887

- George Echlin & Margaret Reid

  - John Echlin – bapt. 2 May 1824 (Baptism, **SS. Michael & John Parish (RC)**)

- George Echlin & Martha Connolly

  o Mary Josephine Echlin – b. 1 Sep 1863, bapt. 8 Sep 1863 (Baptism, **SS. Michael & John Parish (RC)**)

George Echlin (father):

Residence - 1 George's Avenue - September 8, 1863

- George Echlin & Mary Unknown

  o Esther Echlin – bapt. 1839 (Baptism, **St. Andrew Parish** (RC))

- George Echlin & Matilda Ryan – 30 Nov 1848 (Marriage, **St. Nicholas Parish** (RC))

Wedding Witnesses:

Edward Stringer & Elizabeth Keeffe

- George Echlin & Roseanne Williams

  o George Echlin – b. 28 Sep 1853, bapt. 3 Sep 1876 (Baptism, **St. Mary, Pro Cathedral Parish** (RC))

George Echlin (father):

Residence - 3 Stafford Street - September 3, 1876

- George Echlin & Teresa Unknown

  o George Echlin & Catherine Flynn – 3 Oct 1875 (Marriage, **St. Andrew Parish** (RC))

    ▪ Christopher Echlin – b. 1878, bapt. 1878 (Baptism, **St. Andrew Parish** (RC))

    ▪ Mary Teresa Echlin – b. 1880, bapt. 1880 (Baptism, **St. Andrew Parish** (RC))

    ▪ Teresa Echlin – b. 1882, bapt. 1882 (Baptism, **St. Andrew Parish** (RC))

    ▪ Ellen Josephine Echlin – b. 1887, bapt. 1887 (Baptism, **St. Andrew Parish** (RC))

Echlin Surname Ireland: 1600s to 1900s

- Leticia Echlin – b. 6 Aug 1890, bapt. 18 Aug 1890 (Baptism, **SS. Michael & John Parish (RC)**)

George Echlin (son):

    Residence - 2 Clarendon Market - October 3, 1875

        44 South King Street - 1873

        4 Chatham Row - 1880

        3 Clarendon Market - 1882

        19 Lower Mercer Street - 1887

        28 Lower Stephen Street - August 18, 1890

Catherine Flynn, daughter of John Flynn & Ellen Unknown (daughter-in-law):

    Residence - 1 Clarendon Market - October 3, 1875

Wedding Witnesses:

John Keegan & Anne Leigh

- George Fleming Echlin & Unknown
  - John Fleming Echlin & Christina Georgina Anne Hunter Carleton – 1 Mar 1866 (Marriage, **Rathmines Parish**)

Signatures:

- Mildred Fleming Echlin & Richard Andrew Mooney – 1 Jun 1892 (Marriage, **Grangegorman**

  Parish)

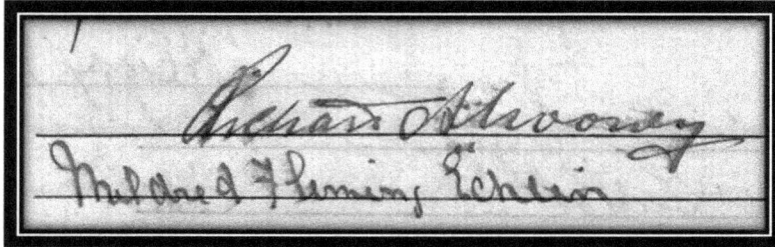

Signatures:

Mildred Fleming Echlin (daughter):

Residence - 35 Nelson Street - June 1, 1892

Richard Andrew Mooney, son of Robert Mooney (son-in-law):

Residence - 1 Rosemont Road - June 1, 1892

Occupation - Ordnance Survey - June 1, 1892

Robert Mooney (father):

Occupation - Ordnance Survey

John Fleming Echlin (father):

Occupation - Gentleman

Echlin Surname Ireland: 1600s to 1900s

Wedding Witnesses:

H. L. Epahaur & B. W. Mooney

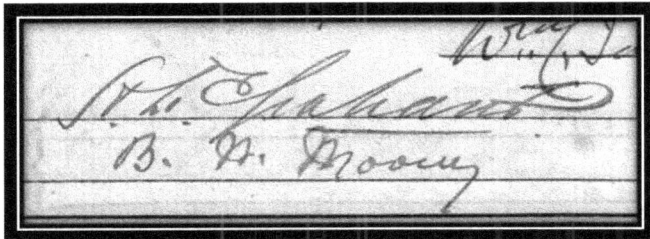

Signatures:

John Fleming Echlin (son):

    Residence - 38 South Cullenswood Avenue - March 1, 1866

    Occupation - Esquire - March 1, 1866

Christina Georgina Anne Hunter Carleton, daughter of Christopher Dorchester Carleton (daughter-in-law):

    Residence - 9 Adelaide Road - March 1, 1866

Christopher Dorchester Carleton (father):

    Occupation - Esquire

George Fleming Echlin (father):

    Occupation - Governor of Jails, Co. Down

Hurst

Wedding Witnesses:

George Hudson & Michael Fenton

Signatures:

- Guy Echlin & Margaret Unknown

    o John Henry Echlin – b. 4 Apr Unclear (Baptism, **St. James Parish**)

Guy Echlin (father):

Residence - James Street - April 4, Unclear

- Guy Cooke Echlin, b. 1834, bur. 6 Apr 1898 (Burial, **St. George Parish**) & Unknown

    o Mary Jane Echlin & Patrick Meighan – 6 Jun 1874 (Marriage, **St. George Parish**)

Signatures:

Mary Jane Echlin (father):

Residence - 83 Lower Dorset Street - June 6, 1874

Echlin Surname Ireland: 1600s to 1900s

Patrick Meighan, son of James Meighan (son-in-law):

    Residence - 83 Lower Dorset Street - June 6, 1874

    Occupation - Civil Engineer - June 6, 1874

James Meighan (father):

    Occupation - Farmer

Guy Cooke Echlin (father):

    Occupation - Gentleman

Wedding Witnesses:

Thomas Rea & Mary Anne Walker

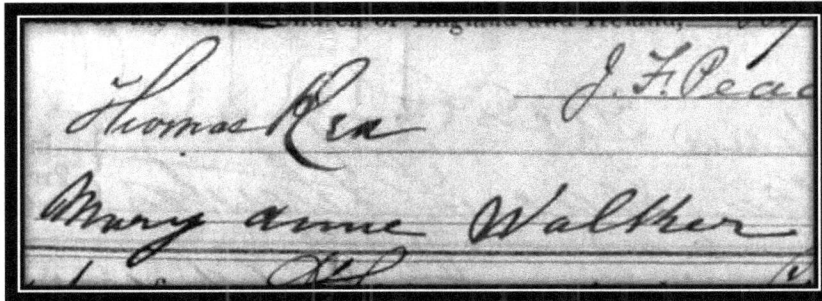

Signatures:

Guy Cooke Echlin (father):

    Residence - 20 Gloucester Street - before April 6, 1898

    Age at Death - 64 years

- Henry Echlin & Elizabeth Millar – Unclear (Marriage, **St. Peter Parish**)

Elizabeth Millar (wife):

    Residence - St. Peter Parish - Unclear

Hurst

- Henry Echlin & Elizabeth Mullen – 25 Feb 1828 (Marriage, **St. Peter Parish**)

Henry Echlin (husband):

Residence - 1 Hatch Street, St. Peter Parish - February 25, 1828

Elizabeth Mullen (wife):

Residence - 1 Hatch Street, St. Peter Parish - February 25, 1828

Wedding Witnesses:

John Unknown & Maria Unknown

- Henry Echlin & Jane Bainter

  o Elizabeth Echlin – bapt. 18 Jan 1867 (Baptism, **St. Mary, Pro Cathedral Parish (RC)**)

Henry Echlin (father):

Residence - Abbey Street - January 18, 1867

- Henry Echlin & Jane Echlin

  o Susanna Echlin – b. 7 Mar 1710, bapt. 20 Mar 1710 (Baptism, **St. Mary Parish**)

  o Jane Echlin – b. 15 Jun 1713, bapt. 26 Jun 1713 (Baptism, **St. Mary Parish**)

Henry Echlin (father):

Occupation - Minister - March 20, 1710

Reverend - June 26, 1713

- Henry Echlin & Louisa Henrietta Espinasse – 5 Jan 1842 (Marriage, **St. Peter Parish**)

Henry Echlin (husband):

Residence - Lower Mount Street - January 5, 1842

Echlin Surname Ireland: 1600s to 1900s

Louisa Henrietta Espinasse (wife):

Residence - Dundrum, Tuney Parish - January 5, 1842

Wedding Witnesses:

Barney Neill & William Espinasse

- Henry Echlin & Rachel Echlin

  - Catherine Echlin – bapt. 7 May 1735 (Baptism, **St. Mary Parish**)

  - Penelope Echlin – bapt. 25 Jun 1736 (Baptism, **St. Mary Parish**)

  - Eleanor Echlin – bapt. 9 Jul 1737 (Baptism, **St. Mary Parish**)

- Henry Echlin & Susanna Echlin

  - Chamberlain Echlin – b. 19 Mar 1712, bapt. 6 Apr 1712 (Baptism, **St. Mary Parish**)

Henry Echlin (father):

Occupation - Reverend - April 6, 1712

- Henry Echlin & Unknown

  - Charles Echlin – bapt. 18 Oct 1679 (Baptism, **St. John Parish**), bur. 22 Dec 1680 (Burial, **St. John Parish**)

- Henry Echlin & Unknown

  - John Echlin – b. 1845, bur. 15 Mar 1849 (Burial, **St. Nicholas Without Parish**)

John Echlin (son):

Residence - Mackey's Terrace - before 15 Mar 1849

Age at Death - 4 years

- Henry Echlin & Unknown

Signature:

- ○ Susan Anne Echlin & John Joseph Mulock – 26 Apr 1861 (Marriage, **St. George Parish**)

Signatures:

Susan Anne Echlin (daughter):

　Residence - **37 Hardwicke Street** - April 26, 1861

　Relationship Status at Marriage - minor

John Joseph Mulock, son of Robert Mulock (son-in-law):

　Residence - Curragh Camp, Co. Kildare - April 26, 1861

　Occupation - Assistant Surgeon, 96th Regiment - April 26, 1861

Robert Mulock (father):

　Occupation - Medical Doctor

Henry Echlin (father):

　Occupation - Esquire

Echlin Surname Ireland: 1600s to 1900s

Wedding Witnesses:

Henry Echlin & Leslie Toke

Signatures:

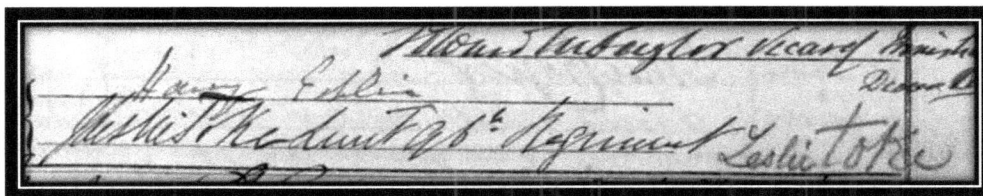

- Henry Echlin & Unknown

  o Henry Echlin & Mary Alice Harrell – 14 Feb 1888 (Marriage, **St. Andrew Parish (RC)**)

Henry Echlin (son):

Residence - 34 Moss Street - February 14, 1888

Mary Alice Harrell, daughter of William Harrell (daughter-in-law):

Residence - 34 Moss Street - February 14, 1888

Wedding Witnesses:

Thomas Blake & Dora Deegan

- Hugh Echlin & Catherine Echlin

  o John Echlin – b. 23 Oct 1709, bapt. 26 Oct 1709 (Baptism, **St. Mary Parish**)

  o Mary Echlin – b. 31 Aug 1711, bapt. 4 Sep 1711 (Baptism, **St. Mary Parish**)

  o Mary Echlin – b. 19 Sep 1712, bapt. 24 Sep 1712 (Baptism, **St. Mary Parish**)

  o Henry Echlin – bapt. 4 Dec 1718 (Baptism, **St. Mary Parish**)

  o Dorothy Echlin – bapt. 27 Nov 1721 (Baptism, **St. Mary Parish**)

Hurst

Hugh Echlin (father):

 Occupation - Joiner - October 26, 1709

    September 4, 1711

    September 24, 1712

- Hugh Thomas Echlin & Unknown
  - Hubert Echlin & Maria Louisa Ward – 28 Apr 1850 (Marriage, **St. Peter Parish**)

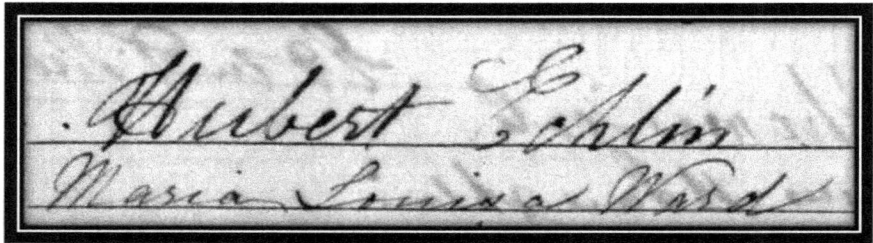

Signatures:

Hubert Echlin (son):

 Residence - Dubber, Santry Parish - April 28, 1850

 Occupation - Gentleman - April 28, 1850

Maria Louisa Ward, daughter of George Ward (daughter-in-law):

 Residence - 19 Camden Street - April 28, 1850

George Ward (father):

 Occupation - Merchant

Hugh Thomas Echlin (father):

 Occupation - Farmer

Echlin Surname Ireland: 1600s to 1900s

Wedding Witnesses:

Thomas Vance & Julia Anne Hervis

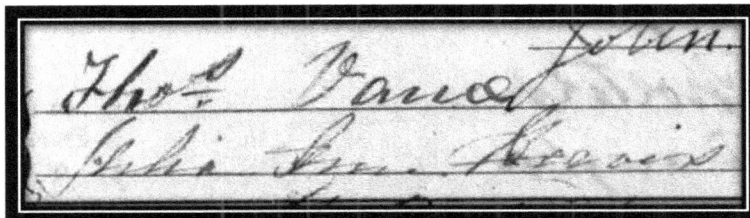

Signatures:

- James Echlin & Mary Unknown

  o Margaret Echlin – bapt. 1804 (Baptism, **St. Andrew Parish (RC)**)

- James Echlin & Mary Anne Sampson – 2 Mar 1733 (Marriage, **St. Mary Parish**)

James Echlin (husband):

Occupation - Esquire - March 2, 1738

- John Echlin & Alice Unknown

  o John Echlin – bapt. 31 Jan 1713 (Baptism, **St. Peter Parish**)

  o William Echlin – bapt. 2 Jan 1715 (Baptism, **St. Peter Parish**), bur. 3 Jun 1717 (Burial, **St. Peter Parish**)

William Echlin (son):

Residence - Stephen's Green - before June 3, 1717

  o Frances Echlin – bapt. 8 Jul 1716 (Baptism, **St. Peter Parish**), bur. 9 Jun 1717 (Burial, **St. Peter Parish**)

Hurst

Frances Echlin (daughter):

Residence - Stephen's Green - before June 9, 1717

- ○ Robert Echlin – bur. 3 Jun 1717 (Burial, **St. Peter Parish**)

Robert Echlin (son):

Residence - Stephen's Green - before June 3, 1717

John Echlin (father):

Residence - Stephen's Green - January 31, 1713

January 2, 1715

Occupation - Reverend - July 8, 1716

- John Echlin & Anne Echlin
  - ○ Anne Echlin – bapt. 8 Dec 1783 (Baptism, **St. Luke Parish**)
  - ○ Charlotte Echlin – bapt. 8 Dec 1783 (Baptism, **St. Luke Parish**)

John Echlin (father):

Residence - Skinner's Alley - December 8, 1783

Occupation - Tape Weaver - December 8, 1783

- John Echlin & Anne Walsh
  - ○ Mary Echlin – bapt. 24 Jan 1814 (Baptism, **St. James Parish (RC)**)
- John Echlin & Catherine Echlin
  - ○ Catherine Echlin – bapt. 18 Apr 1707 (Baptism, **St. Catherine Parish**)
  - ○ Mary Echlin – bapt. 29 May 1711 (Baptism, **St. Catherine Parish**)

Echlin Surname Ireland: 1600s to 1900s

- John Echlin & Catherine Echlin

  - Guy Cooke Echlin – bapt. 20 Dec 1798 (Baptism, **St. Paul Parish**)

- John Echlin & Catherine Unknown

  - Alice Echlin – b. 1807, bapt. 16 Feb 1807 (Baptism, **St. Catherine Parish**)

- John Echlin & Eleanor Unknown

  - Mary Anne Echlin – bapt. 25 Jul 1790 (Baptism, **St. Werburgh Parish**)

  - Sabine Evelyn Echlin – bapt. 6 May 1792 (Baptism, **St. Werburgh Parish**)

John Echlin (father):

Residence - Castle Street - July 25, 1790

Hoey's Court - May 6, 1792

- John Echlin & Elizabeth Echlin

  - Mary Anne Echlin – b. 7 Aug 1822, bapt. 26 Aug 1822 (Baptism, **St. Mary Parish**)

John Echlin (father):

Residence - 16 Moore Street - August 26, 1822

- John Echlin & Elizabeth Groves

  - Anne Echlin – bapt. 11 Feb 1776 (Baptism, **St. Catherine Parish** (RC))

  - Elizabeth Echlin – bapt. 14 Jun 1778 (Baptism, **St. Catherine Parish** (RC))

- John Echlin & Elizabeth Unknown

  - John Michael Echlin – bapt. 30 Sep 1827 (Baptism, **St. Mary, Pro Cathedral Parish** (RC))

  - John Echlin – bapt. 7 Aug 1829 (Baptism, **St. Mary, Pro Cathedral Parish** (RC))

- John Echlin & Hester Echlin

  - John Echlin – bapt. 23 Mar 1757 (Baptism, **St. Mary Parish**)

Hurst

John Echlin (father):

Occupation - Esquire - March 23, 1757

- John Echlin & Jane Echlin
  - John Pedder Echlin – b. 28 Nov 1837, bapt. 30 Nov 1837 (Baptism, **St. George Parish**)

John Echlin (father):

Residence - No. 27 Nelson Street - November 30, 1837

Occupation - Barrister at Law - November 30, 1837

- John Echlin & Mary Echlin
  - Arthur John Echlin – b. 4 Jul 1870, bapt. 24 Jul 1870 (Baptism, **St. Peter Parish**)

John Echlin (father):

Residence - Raglan House, Clyde Road - July 24, 1870

Occupation - Clerk - July 24, 1870

- John Echlin & Mary Mitchell – 25 Sep 1725 (Marriage, **St. Mary Parish**)
- John Echlin & Mary O'Neill
  - Margaret Echlin – bapt. 12 Aug 1805 (Baptism, **St. Catherine Parish (RC)**)
- John Echlin & Mary Unknown
  - Mary Rebecca Echlin – bapt. 1843 (Baptism, **St. Andrew Parish (RC)**)
- John Echlin & Melissa Echlin
  - Charles Echlin – bapt. 9 Sep 1802 (Baptism, **St. Catherine Parish**)

John Echlin (father):

Residence - Portland Street - September 9, 1802

Echlin Surname Ireland: 1600s to 1900s

- John Echlin & Unknown

  - Margaret Echlin & Alexander Cranston – 22 Nov 1845 (Marriage, **St. Peter Parish**)

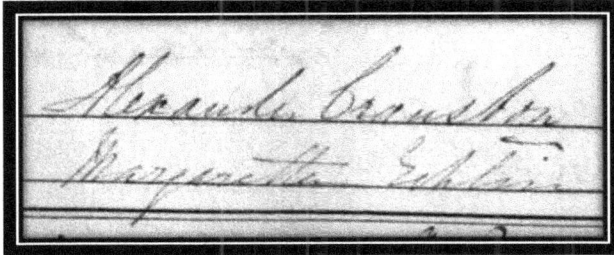

Signatures:

Margaret Echlin (daughter):

Residence - Brougham Place - November 22, 1845

Alexander Cranston, son of John Cranston (son-in-law):

Residence - Down Parish - November 22, 1845

Occupation - Esquire - November 22, 1845

John Cranston (father):

Occupation - Esquire

John Echlin (father):

Occupation - Esquire

Hurst

Wedding Witnesses:

Charles Echlin & George Alexander

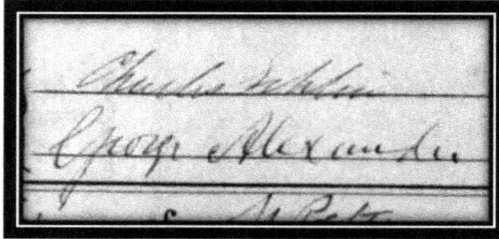

Signatures:

- John Echlin & Unknown
  - Harriet Echlin & Henry Perceval – 1 May 1850 (Marriage, **St. Peter Parish**)

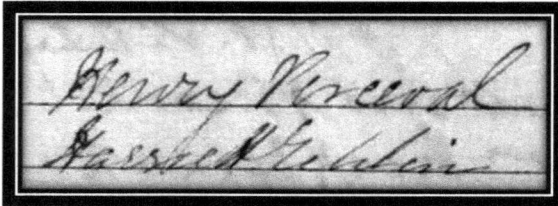

Signatures:

Harriet Echlin (daughter):

    Residence - 9 Heytesbury Terrace, St. Peter Parish - May 1, 1850

Henry Perceval, son of William Perceval (son-in-law):

    Residence - 32 South Frederick Street, St. Anne Parish - May 1, 1850

    Occupation - Esquire - May 1, 1850

William Perceval (father):

    Occupation - Captain in Army

Echlin Surname Ireland: 1600s to 1900s

John Echlin (father):

    Occupation - Esquire

Wedding Witnesses:

W. Echlin & Edmund John Armstrong

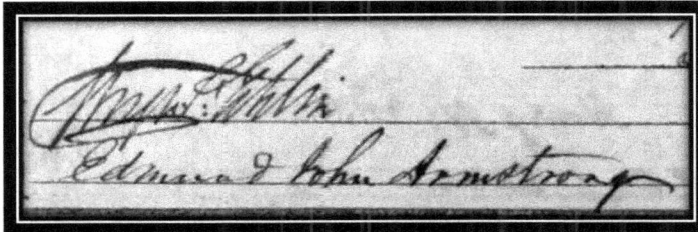

Signatures:

- John Godfrey Echlin & Anne Medici Echlin

  o Godfrey Cecil Echlin – b. 12 Aug 1874, bapt. 30 Sep 1874 (Baptism, **St. George Parish**)

John Godfrey Echlin (father):

    Residence - North Frederick Street - September 30, 1874

    Occupation - Esquire - September 30, 1874

- John Harold Echlin & Harriet Echlin

  o Harriet Maria Echlin – bapt. 24 Jul 1836 (Baptism, **St. Paul Parish**)

- John Henry Echlin & Mary Unknown

  o John Henry Echlin – b. 4 Aug 1849, bapt. 5 Jul 1854 (Baptism, **St. Peter Parish**)

  o Mary Echlin – b. 18 Aug 1853, bapt. 5 Jul 1854 (Baptism, **St. Peter Parish**)

  o Harriet Jane Echlin – b. 3 Nov 1867, bapt. 3 Mar 1868 (Baptism, **St. Catherine Parish**)

John Henry Echlin (father):

Residence - 24 Upper Leeson Street - July 5, 1854

2 Market Street - 1868

Occupation - Cabinet Maker - July 5, 1854

1868

- Matthew Echlin & Unknown
  - o Maria Echlin & William Robert Adams – 11 Jun 1874 (Marriage, **Rathmines Parish**)

Signatures:

Maria Echlin (daughter):

Residence - 12 Richmond Street - June 11, 1874

William Robert Adams, son of Abraham Adams (son-in-law):

Residence - 12 Richmond Street - June 11, 1874

Occupation - Esquire - June 11, 1874

Abraham Adams (father):

Occupation - Esquire

Matthew Echlin (father):

Occupation - Carpenter

Echlin Surname Ireland: 1600s to 1900s

Wedding Witnesses:

John Langton, Sarah Adams, & Elizabeth Morris

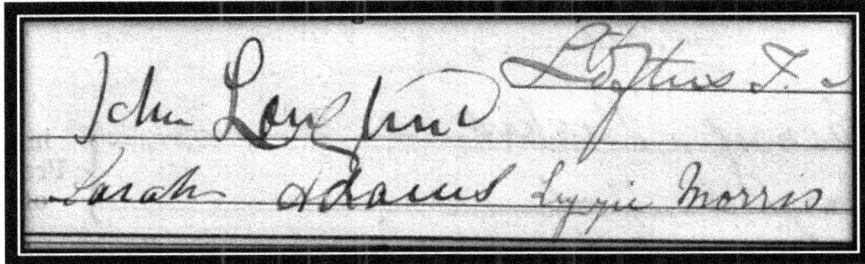

Signatures:

- Michael Echlin & Alice Corry – 9 Aug 1756 (Marriage, **St. Mary Parish**)

  o Alice Echlin – bapt. 30 Mar 1763 (Baptism, **St. Mary Parish**)

- Paul Echlin & Anne Echlin

  o John Echlin – bapt. 25 Jan 1741 (Baptism, **St. Catherine Parish**)

- Paul Echlin & Anne Unknown

  o Henry Echlin – bapt. 25 Jan 1762 (Baptism, **St. Catherine Parish (RC)**)

- Ralph Echlin & Jane Unknown

  o Mary Echlin – bapt. 2 Sep 1747 (Baptism, **St. Catherine Parish (RC)**)

- Richard Echlin & Mary Unknown

  o Elizabeth Echlin – bapt. 4 Nov 1716 (Baptism, **St. Nicholas Without Parish**)

Richard Echlin (father):

Residence - The Coombe - before November 4, 1716

- Robert Echlin & Anne Unknown

  o Frances or Francis Echlin – bapt. 11 Mar 1760 (Baptism, **St. Catherine Parish**)

Hurst

- Robert Echlin & Catherine Cannon – 29 Jan 1752 (Marriage, **St. Mary Parish**)

Robert Echlin (husband):

Residence - Drumlatery, Co. Dublin - January 29, 1752

- Robert Echlin & Elizabeth Echlin
  - Elizabeth Echlin – b. 6 Sep 1728, bapt. 26 Sep 1728 (Baptism, **St. Mary Parish**)
- Robert Echlin, bur. 23 Dec 1706 (Burial, **St. John Parish**) & Penelope Unknown
  - Anne Echlin – bapt. 4 Oct 1698 (Baptism, **St. Mary Parish**), bur. 28 Dec 1699 (Burial, **St. John Parish**)
  - Robert Echlin – bapt. 4 Dec 1699 (Baptism, **St. Mary Parish**)
  - Frances Echlin – bapt. 23 Feb 1700 (Baptism, **St. Mary Parish**)
  - Agnes Echlin – bapt. 14 May 1702 (Baptism, **St. Mary Parish**), bur. 31 May 1702 (Burial, **St. John Parish**)
  - Anne Echlin – bapt. 14 May 1702 (Baptism, **St. Mary Parish**)
  - Henry Echlin – b. 14 Jun 1703, bapt. 22 Jun 1703 (Baptism, **St. Mary Parish**)
  - Eustace Echlin – bur. 23 Jun 1704 (Burial, **St. John Parish**)
  - Penelope Echlin – bur. 2 Aug 1707 (Burial, **St. John Parish**)
  - Frances Echlin – bur. 23 Dec 1708 (Burial, **St. John Parish**)

Robert Echlin (father):

Occupation - Esquire - October 4, 1698

December 4, 1699

June 23, 1704

Before December 23, 1706

Echlin Surname Ireland: 1600s to 1900s

Gentleman - May 14, 1702

June 22, 1703

- Roger Echlin & Anne Macken – 5 Jan 1794 (Marriage, **St. Catherine Parish**)

- Thomas Echlin & Elizabeth Echlin

  - Christopher Echlin – bapt. 7 Nov 1742 (Baptism, **Tullow Parish**)

- Thomas Echlin & Leticia Echlin

  - Thomas Echlin – bapt. 26 Apr 1720 (Baptism, **St. Audoen Parish**)

- Thomas Echlin & Mary Unknown

  - Anne Echlin – bapt. 13 Jan 1760 (Baptism, **St. Michan Parish (RC)**)

- Thomas Echlin & Rachel Echlin

  - John Echlin – bapt. 1 Jun 1731 (Baptism, **St. Catherine Parish**)

- Unknown Echlin & Anne Unknown

  - Harriet Echlin – bapt. 20 May 1810 (Baptism, **St. John Parish**)

Unknown Echlin (father):

Occupation - Chamberlain - May 20, 1810

- Unknown Echlin & Elizabeth Echlin, bur. 28 Sep 1695 (Burial, **St. John Parish**)

Unknown Echlin (husband):

Occupation - Colonel - September 28, 1695

- Unknown Echlin & Grizel Unknown

  - Unknown Echlin – bapt. Sep 1722 (Baptism, **St. John Parish**)

Hurst

Unknown Echlin (father):

Residence - Unknown Court - September 1722

Occupation - Gentleman - September 1722

- Unknown Echlin & Susan Echlin
  - William Echlin – b. 31 Dec 1893, bapt. 7 Jan 1894 (Baptism, **Rotunda Chapel Parish**)

Susan Echlin (mother):

Residence - 33 Lower Gardiner Street - January 7, 1894

Occupation - Domestic Servant - January 7, 1894

- Unknown Echlin & Unknown
  - Unknown Echlin (Son or Daughter) – bur. 2 Jan 1685 (Burial, **St. John Parish**)

Unknown Echlin (son or daughter):

Age at Death - child

- Unknown Echlin & Unknown
  - Unknown (Son or Daughter) – bur. 8 Oct 1765 (Burial, **St. Mary Parish**)

Unknown Echlin (son or daughter):

Residence - Dorset Street - before October 8, 1765

Age At Death - child

  - Unknown (Son or Daughter) – bur. 12 Dec 1765 (Burial, **St. Mary Parish**)

Echlin Surname Ireland: 1600s to 1900s

Unknown Echlin (son or daughter):

    Residence - Dorset Street - before December 12, 1765

    Age At Death - child

Unknown Echlin (father):

    Residence - Dorset Street - October 8, 1765

        December 12, 1765

- Unknown Echlin & Unknown
  - Elizabeth Echlin

Signature:

- Unknown Echlin & Unknown
  - Jane Echlin

Signature:

- Unknown Echlin & Unknown
  - Lydia Echlin

Signature:

- Unknown Echlin & Unknown

  o Robert Echlin

Robert Echlin (son):

Occupation - Barrister

o Henry Echlin, d. 16 Oct 1740, bur. 18 Oct 1740 (Burial, **St. John Parish**) & Rachel Echlin, d. 22 Dec 1740, bur. 24 Dec 1740 (Burial, **St. John Parish**)

  ▪ Henry Echlin – b. 22 Dec 1740, bapt. 5 Jan 1741 (Baptism, **St. Mary Parish**)

Henry Echlin (son):

Occupation - Esquire - October 16, 1740

before January 5, 1741

- William Echlin & Alice Echlin

  o Charles James Echlin – bapt. 28 Jul 1758 (Baptism, **St. Mary Parish**)

- William Echlin & Mary Unknown

  o Anne Echlin – b. 1765, bapt. 30 Jun 1765 (Baptism, **St. Catherine Parish** (RC))

  o Anne Echlin – b. 1767, bapt. 26 Jul 1767 (Baptism, **St. Catherine Parish** (RC))

- William Echlin & Unknown

  o Anne Echlin – bapt. 27 Feb 1622 (Baptism, **St. John Parish**), bur. 27 Dec 1623 (Burial, **St. John Parish**)

  o Anne Echlin – bapt. 18 Nov 1624 (Baptism, **St. John Parish**)

  o Ursula Echlin – bapt. 8 Apr 1630 (Baptism, **St. John Parish**)

  o Judith Echlin – bapt. 27 Jun 1631 (Baptism, **St. John Parish**)

  o Jane Echlin – bapt. 3 Aug 1633 (Baptism, **St. John Parish**)

Echlin Surname Ireland: 1600s to 1900s

- o   John Echlin – bapt. 3 Aug 1633 (Baptism, **St. John Parish**)

- o   William Echlin – bapt. 5 Apr 1635 (Baptism, **St. John Parish**)

- William Frederick Echlin & Mary Anne Beckett

  - o   Catherine Margaret Echlin – b. 19 Oct 1852, bapt. 27 Oct 1852 (Baptism, **St. Werburgh Parish**)

  - o   William Frederick Echlin – b. 11 Jan 1858, bapt. 2 Feb 1858 (Baptism, **St. Michan Parish** (RC))

  - o   William Frederick Echlin – b. 11 Jan 1859, bapt. 6 Feb 1859 (Baptism, **St. Mary Parish**)

  - o   Elizabeth Echlin – b. 9 Jun 1861, bapt. 19 Jun 1861 (Baptism, **St. Michan Parish** (RC))

  - o   Mary Anne Echlin – b. 27 Nov 1863, bapt 30 Nov 1863 (Baptism, **St. Michan Parish** (RC))

  - o   Charles Thomas Echlin – b. 10 Oct 1865, bapt. 13 Oct 1865 (Baptism, **St. Michan Parish** (RC))

  - o   Edward Echlin & Elizabeth Byrne (B y r n e) – 3 May 1885 (Marriage, **St. Mary, Pro Cathedral Parish** (RC))

Edward Echlin (son):

Residence - 39 Capel Street - May 3, 1885

Elizabeth Byrne, daughter of Luke Byrne & Margaret Maher (daughter-in-law):

Residence - 39 Capel Street - May 3, 1885

Wedding Witnesses:

Patrick Byrne & Teresa Byrne

William Fredrick Echlin (father):

Residence - 17 New Row - October 27, 1852

186 North King Street - February 2, 1858

February 6, 1859

Hurst

June 19, 1861

November 30, 1863

187 King Street - October 13, 1865

Occupation - Paper Stainer - October 27, 1852

February 6, 1859

Individual Baptisms/Births

- John Echlin – bapt. 19 Sep 1805 (Baptism, **St. Catherine Parish (RC)**)

John Echlin (child):

　Remarks about Birth - foundling

Individual Burials

- Alice Echlin – bur. 15 Dec 1804 (Burial, **St. Peter Parish**)

Alice Echlin (deceased):

    Residence - Stephen's Green - before December 15, 1804

- Alice Echlin – bur. 13 Apr 1805 (Burial, **St. Peter Parish**)

Alice Echlin (deceased):

    Residence - Stephen's Green - before April 13, 1805

- Anne Echlin – bur. 26 Aug 1813 (Burial, **St. Mary Parish**)

Anne Echlin (deceased):

    Residence - Sackville Street - before August 26, 1813

    Relationship Status at Death - Miss

- Anne Phyllis Echlin – b. 1761, bur. 3 May 1852 (Burial, **St. Mary Parish**)

Anne Phyllis Echlin (deceased):

    Residence - 99 Lower Mount Street - before May 3, 1852

    Age at Death - 91 years

- Brabston Echlin – bur. 4 Nov 1717 (Burial, **St. Catherine Parish**)

Echlin Surname Ireland: 1600s to 1900s

- Catherine Echlin – bur. 10 Jul 1815 (Burial, **St. Mary Parish**)

Catherine Echlin (deceased):

    Residence - Merrion - before July 10, 1815

    Relationship Status at Death - Mrs.

- Catherine Echlin – b. 1814, bur. 8 Jan 1818 (Burial, **St. Mary Parish**)

Catherine Echlin (deceased):

    Age at Death - 4 years

- Charles Moore Echlin – b. 1794, bur. 7 Jun 1848 (Burial, **St. Mary Parish**)

Charles Moore Echlin (deceased):

    Residence - Killinah Glebe, Co. Cavan - before June 7, 1848

    Age at Death - 54 Years

- E. Echlin – b. 1792, bur. 21 Feb 1837 (Burial, **St. George Parish**)

E. Echlin (deceased):

    Residence - Rutland Lane - before February 21, 1837

    Age at Death - 45 years

- Edward Echlin – bur. 17 Apr 1736 (Burial, **St. Catherine Parish**)
- Elizabeth Echlin – bur. Sep 1702 (Burial, **St. Nicholas Without Parish**)

Elizabeth Echlin (deceased):

    Residence - Truck Street - before September 1702

- Elizabeth Echlin – bur. 7 Feb 1718 (Burial, **St. Mary Parish**)

Elizabeth Echlin (deceased):

    Relationship Status at Death - widow

- Elizabeth Echlin – b. 1793, bur. 19 Feb 1840 (Burial, **St. Peter Parish**)

Elizabeth Echlin (deceased):

    Residence - Mount Street - before February 19, 1840

    Age at Death - 47 years

    Place of Burial - St. Kevin's Cemetery - February 19, 1840

- Elizabeth Echlin – b. 1789, bur. 14 Mar 1841 (Burial, **St. Mary Parish**)

Elizabeth Echlin (deceased):

    Residence - Lower Mount Street - before March 14, 1841

    Age at Death - 52 years

- Emily Echlin – b. 1805, bur. 16 Aug 1833 (Burial, **St. Mary Parish**)

Emily Echlin (deceased):

    Residence - Mount Street - before August 16, 1833

    Age at Death - 28 Years

- Esther Echlin – bur. 9 Feb 1801 (Burial, **St. Catherine Parish**)
- Esther Echlin – b. 21 Feb 1839, bur. 6 Mar 1839 (Burial, **St. Peter Parish**)

Echlin Surname Ireland: 1600s to 1900s

Esther Echlin (deceased):

    Residence - Digges Lane - before March 6, 1839

    Age at Death - 2 weeks

    Place of Burial - St. Kevin's Cemetery - March 6, 1839

- Harriet Echlin – b. 1836, bur. 12 Jun 1846 (Burial, **St. Mark Parish**)

Harriet Echlin (deceased):

    Residence - Townsend Street - before June 12, 1846

    Age at Death - 10 years

- Henrietta Echlin – bur. 8 Nov 1793 (Burial, **St. Paul Parish**)
- Henry Echlin – bur. 1 Dec 1725 (Burial, **St. John Parish**)

Henry Echlin (deceased):

    Occupation - Knight - before December 1, 1725

- Henry Echlin – bur. 4 Aug 1815 (Burial, **St. Mary Parish**)

Henry Echlin (deceased):

    Residence - Booterstown - before August 4, 1815

- James Echlin – b. 1807, bur. 9 Jul 1832 (Burial, **St. Mary Parish**)

James Echlin (deceased):

    Residence - William's Town - before July 9, 1832

    Age at Death - 25 years

- Jane Echlin – bur. 21 Sep 1734 (Burial, **St. Nicholas Without Parish**)

Jane Echlin (deceased):

> **Residence - Patrick Street - before September 21, 1734**

- Jane Echlin – bur. 11 Sep 1770 (Burial, **St. Catherine Parish**)

- Jane Echlin – b. 1806, bur. 27 Mar 1886 (Burial, **St. George Parish**)

Jane Echlin (deceased):

> **Residence - 110 Lower Dorset Street - before March 27, 1886**

> **Age at Death - 80 years**

- John Echlin – bur. 13 Jun 1726 (Burial, **St. John Parish**)

- John Echlin – bur. 13 Jul 1726 (Burial, **St. John Parish**)

- John Echlin – b. 1789, bur. 16 Apr 1842 (Burial, **St. Mary Parish**)

John Echlin (deceased):

> **Residence - Frescati, Black Rock - before April 16, 1842**

> **Age at Death - 53 years**

- John Henry Echlin – b. 1815, d. 5 Jul 1869, bur. 1869 (Burial, **St. James Parish**)

John Henry Echlin (deceased):

> **Residence - 169 James Street - July 5, 1869**

> **Age at Death - 54 years**

Echlin Surname Ireland: 1600s to 1900s

- Margery Echlin – b. 1697, bur. 18 Feb 1757 (Burial, **St. Werburgh Parish**)

Margery Echlin (deceased):

Residence - Hoey's Court - before February 18, 1757

Age at Death - 60 years

Cause of Death - decay

Relationship Status at Death - Mrs.

- Mary Echlin – b. 1851, bur. 25 Mar 1853 (Burial, **St. Nicholas Without Parish**)

Mary Echlin (deceased):

Residence - Leeson Street - before March 25, 1853

Age at Death - 2 years

- Moore Echlin – bur. 31 Mar 1821 (Burial, **Carlow Parish**)
- Moore Echlin – b. 1829, bur. 21 Feb 1847 (Burial, **St. Mary Parish**)

Moore Echlin (deceased):

Residence - Mount Street - before February 21, 1847

Age at Death - 18 years

- Ralph Echlin – bur. 19 Dec 1769 (Burial, **St. Catherine Parish**)
- Robert Echlin – bur. 4 Apr 1736 (Burial, **St. Catherine Parish**)

Hurst

- Robert Echlin – bur. 11 Jul 1801 (Burial, **St. Catherine Parish**)

Robert Echlin (deceased):

    Residence - Harold's Cross - before July 11, 1801

- Robert Echlin – bur. 17 Jan 1809 (Burial, **St. Mary Parish**)

Robert Echlin (deceased):

    Residence - Francis Street - January 17, 1809

- Robert Echlin – bur. 19 Oct 1816 (Burial, **St. Mark Parish**)
- Robert Echlin – bur. 21 Sep Unclear (Burial, **Carlow Parish**)
- Susannah Echlin – bur. 25 Jul 1723 (Burial, **St. Catherine Parish**)

Susannah Echlin (deceased):

    Age at Death - child

- Thomas Echlin – b. 1772, bur. 8 Jul 1732 (Burial, **St. Mary Parish**)

Thomas Echlin (deceased):

    Residence - William's Town - before July 8, 1732

    Age at Death - 60 years

- Thomasina M. Echlin – b. 1788, bur. 22 Jan 1851 (Burial, **St. Mary Parish**)

Thomasina M. Echlin (deceased):

    Residence - 9 Heytesbury Terrace - before January 22, 1851

    Age at Death - 63 years

Echlin Surname Ireland: 1600s to 1900s

- Unknown Echlin – bur. 6 May 1718 (Burial, St. Nicholas Without Parish)

Unknown Echlin (deceased):

   Residence - The Coombe - before May 6, 1718

- Unknown Echlin – bur. 28 Jan 1735 (Burial, St. John Parish)

- Unknown Echlin – bur. 7 Jun 1764 (Burial, St. John Parish)

- Unknown Echlin (Miss) – bur. 18 Nov 1801 (Burial, St. Audoen Parish)

- Unknown Echlin (Mr.) – bur. 6 Jun 1789 (Burial, St. Mary Parish)

Unknown Echlin (Mr.):

   Residence - Drumcondra - before June 6, 1789

- Unknown Echlin (Mrs.) – bur. 3 Jan 1772 (Burial, St. Mary Parish)

Unknown Echlin (Mrs.):

   Residence - Britain Street - before January 3, 1772

- Unknown Echlin (Mrs.) – bur. 6 Jun 1793 (Burial, St. Mary Parish)

Unknown Echlin (Mrs.):

   Residence - Bolton Street - before June 6, 1793

- Unknown Echlin (Mrs.) – bur. 29 Dec 1804 (Burial, St. Mary Parish)

Unknown Echlin (Mrs.):

   Residence - Church Street - before December 29, 1804

Hurst

- Unknown Echlin (Mrs.) – bur. 18 Feb 1806 (Burial, **St. Mary Parish**)

Unknown Echlin (Mrs.):

  Residence - Abbey Street - before February 18, 1806

- Unknown Echlin (Mrs.) – bur. 11 Jan 1814 (Burial, **St. Mary Parish**)

Unknown Echlin (Mrs.):

  Residence - Fitzwilliam Street - before January 11, 1814

- William Echlin – b. 1 Jan 1894, bur. 12 Jan 1894 (Burial, **St. George Parish**)

William Echlin (deceased):

  Residence - 2 St. Joseph's Terrace - before January 12, 1894

  Age at Death - 12 days

Individual Marriages

- Anne Echlin & John Seward – 11 Jun 1726 (Marriage, **St. Michan Parish**)

John Seward (husband):

   Occupation - Instrument Maker - June 11, 1726

- Anne Echlin & Matthew Dawson – 18 Feb 1640 (Marriage, **St. John Parish**)
- Catherine Echlin & Michael McDonough – Jan 1764 (Marriage, **St. Catherine Parish (RC)**)

Wedding Witnesses:

Bridget Vaughan & Elizabeth Kelly

- Catherine Echlin & Thomas Noonan

   o   Bridget Noonan – b. 1 Feb 1865, bapt. 3 Feb 1865 (Baptism, **St. Nicholas Parish (RC)**)

Thomas Noonan (father):

   Residence - 12 Kevin Street - February 3, 1865

- Eleanor Echlin & James Reynolds

   o   John Reynolds & Mary Anne Sarsfield – 13 Nov 1867 (Marriage, **St. Lawrence Parish (RC)**)

John Reynolds (son):

   Residence - 11 Talbot Place - November 18, 1867

Mary Anne Sarsfield, daughter of Christopher Sarsfield & Mary Duff

(daughter-in-law):

Hurst

Residence - 8 [Hard to Read] **Cottages - November 18, 1867**

Wedding Witnesses:

Charles McCullagh & Emily Sarsfield

- Elizabeth Echlin & Thomas Lawler – 31 Oct 1834 (Marriage, **St. Mary, Pro Cathedral Parish (RC)**)

Wedding Witnesses:

Anthony Connor & Catherine McDonnell

- Jane Echlin & Alexander McLane – 5 Jan 1745 (Marriage, **St. Michan Parish**)
- Juliet Echlin & Michael Boyle – 13 Sep 1795 (Marriage, **St. Bride Parish**)

Michael Boyle (husband):

   Residence - City of Dublin - September 13, 1795

   Occupation - Cutler - September 13, 1795

- Lucretia Echlin & Lawrence Flood
  - Mary Flood – bapt. 1773 (Baptism, **SS. Michael & John Parish (RC)**)
  - John Flood – bapt. 1774 (Baptism, **SS. Michael & John Parish (RC)**)
  - Alice Flood – bapt. 1775 (Baptism, **SS. Michael & John Parish (RC)**)
- Margaret Echlin & John Coyle
  - John Coyle – bapt. 27 Oct 1848 (Baptism, **St. Nicholas Parish (RC)**)
- Margaret Echlin & Robert Howe
  - Sarah Howe – bapt. 7 Apr 1843 (Baptism, **St. Catherine Parish (RC)**)

Echlin Surname Ireland: 1600s to 1900s

- Maria Echlin & John Magrath – 6 Nov 1837 (Marriage, **Grangegorman Parish**)

Signatures:

Mary Echlin (wife):

    Residence - Grangegorman Parish - November 6, 1837

John Magrath (husband):

    Residence - Grangegorman Parish - November 6, 1837

Wedding Witnesses:

John Henry Echlin & Charles Loughry

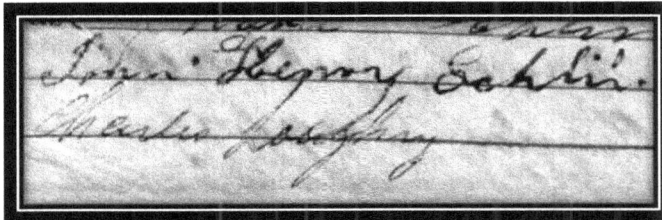

Signatures:

- Mary Echlin & Francis Pullin
  - John Pullin – bapt. 6 Mar 1815 (Baptism, **St. Catherine Parish** (RC))
- Mary Echlin & Garret Walsh – 24 Sep 1806 (Marriage, **St. Mary, Pro Cathedral Parish** (RC))

Wedding Witnesses:

William Johnston & Anne Johnston

- Mary Echlin & James Whittaker

  o George Whittaker – bapt. 28 Jul 1845 (Baptism, **St. Nicholas Parish** (RC))

- Mary Echlin & Mark Anthony McLoughlin

  o Mary McLoughlin – bapt. 13 Mar 1772 (Baptism, **St. Catherine Parish** (RC))

- Mary Echlin & Patrick Russell

  o Thomas Russell & Ellen Keely – 13 Oct 1889 (Marriage, **Rathmines Parish** (RC))

Thomas Russell (son):

Residence - Lock House, Charlemont Bridge - October 13, 1889

Ellen Keely, daughter of James Keely & Mary Reilly (daughter-in-law):

Residence - 4 Dunne's Terrace - October 13, 1889

Wedding Witnesses:

James Keely & Mary Hennessy

- Mary Anne Echlin & James Brophy – 2 Sep 1851 (Marriage, **St. Michan Parish** (RC))

Wedding Witnesses:

James [Hard to Read] & Christopher Timmins

- Sabina Echlin & Lawrence Tomkinson – 26 Nov 1814 (Marriage, **St. Mark Parish**)

  o Mary A. Elizabeth Tomkinson – bapt. 19 Jan 1819 (Baptism, **SS. Michael & John Parish** (RC))

  o Mary Frances Tomkinson – bapt. 8 Jul 1821 (Baptism, **SS. Michael & John Parish** (RC))

  o Mary Elizabeth Tomkinson – bapt. 5 Oct 1823 (Baptism, **SS. Michael & John Parish** (RC))

  o Sabina Tomkinson – bapt. 3 Jul 1826 (Baptism, **SS. Michael & John Parish** (RC))

  o Martha Tomkinson – bapt. Aug 1829 (Baptism, **SS. Michael & John Parish** (RC))

Echlin Surname Ireland: 1600s to 1900s

- Teresa Echlin & Patrick McCarthy

  o Thomas Christopher McCarthy – b. 1883, bapt. 1883 (Baptism, **St. Andrew Parish** (RC))

  o Bridget McCarthy – b. 1886, bapt. 1886 (Baptism, **St. Andrew Parish** (RC))

  o John Joseph McCarthy – b. 1888, bapt. 1888 (Baptism, **St. Andrew Parish** (RC))

Patrick McCarthy (father):

Residence - 7 Clarence Place - 1883

12 Sandwith Street - 1886

Townsend Street - 1888

Name Variations

Includes Latin and Abbreviated forms of names found in the original documents.

Abigail = Abigale, Abigall

Anne = Ann, Anna, Annae

Bartholomew = Barth, Bartholmeus, Bartholomeo

Bridget = Birgis, Brigid, Brigida, Bridgit

Catherine = Catharine, Catharina, Catharinae, Catherina, Cath, Catha, Cathae, Cathe, Cathn, Kate

Charles = Carolus, Charls, Chas

Christopher = Christoph

Daniel = Danielem, Danielis

Edmund = Edmond

Edward = Ed, Edwd

Eleanor = Eleo, Eleonora, Elinor, Ellenor

Elizabeth = Betty, Elisa, Elisabeth, Eliz, Eliza, Elizab, Elizh, Elizth

Ellen = Elena, Ellena

Emily = Emilia

Esther = Essie, Ester

Francis = Fransicum

George = Geo, Georg, Georgius

Grace = Gratiae

Gulielmo = Guil, Guillelmi, Gulielmum, Guillelmus, Gulmi

Helen = Helena

Echlin Surname Ireland: 1600s to 1900s

Honor = Hanora, Honora

James = Jacobi, Jacobus, Jas

Jane = Joanna

Jeanne = Jeannae, Joannae

Joan = Johanna, Joney

John = Jno, Joannem, Joannes, Johannis

Joseph = Jos

Juliana = Julian

Leticia = Letitia, Lettice, Letticia

Lewis = Louis

Luke = Lucas

Margaret = Margarita, Margaritae, Margeret, Marget, Margt

Martha = Marthae

Mary = Maria, My

Mary Anne = Marianna, Marianne, Maryanne

Michael = Michaelis, Michl

Patrick = Pat, Patt, Patk, Patricii, Patricius

Peter = Petri

Richard = Ricardi, Ricardus, Rich, Richd

Robert = Roberti

Rose = Rosa, Rosae

Thomas = Thom, Thomae, Thoms, Thos, Ths

Timothy = Timotheus, Timy

William = Wil, Will, Willm, Wm

Notes

Notes

Notes

Notes

Notes

Notes

Index

Echlin Surname Ireland: 1600s to 1900s

Anne
- *1622 Feb 27* 38
- *1624 Nov 18* 38
- *1698 Oct 4* 34
- *1702 May 14* 34
- *1760 Jan 13* 35
- *1765 Jun 30* 38
- *1767 Jul 26* 38
- *1776 Feb 11* 27
- *1783 Dec 8* 26
- *1891 Sep 25* 7

Arthur John
- *1870 Jul 24* 28

Bridget
- *1743 Nov 20* 11

Catherine
- *1707 Apr 18* 26
- *1735 May 7* 21
- *1783 Jul 28* 1
- *1789 Apr 21* 1
- *1819 May 28* 5
- *1844* 13
- *1887 Mar 2* 13

Catherine Margaret
- *1852 Oct 27* 39

Cecil Moore
- *1882 Jul 2* 7
- *1882 Jun 28* 7

Chamberlin
- *1712 Apr 6* 21

Charles
- *1679 Oct 18* 21
- *1708 Mar 24* 3
- *1758 Jul 28* 38
- *1802 Sep 9* 28

Charles John
- *1881 Feb 4* 13

Charles John Cavendish
- *1895 Mar 10* 2

Charles Thomas
- *1865 Oct 13* 39

Charlotte
- *1783 Dec 8* 26

Charlotte Mary

- *1881 Dec 14* 9

Christopher
- *1700 Nov 21* 3
- *1726 Apr 10* 3
- *1742 Nov 7* 35
- *1878* 14

Daniel Moore
- *1806 Dec 21* 11

Dorothy
- *1721 Nov 27* 23

Edward
- *1817 Jun 21* 5

Edward Joseph
- *1891 Sep 25* 7

Edward Moore
- *1849 Sep 9* 6

Eleanor
- *1737 Jul 9* 21
- *1853 Aug 17* 6
- *1880 May 27* 7

Eleanor Evelyn
- *1882 Jul 2* 7

Elizabeth
- *1703 Aug 1* 3
- *1710 Aug 10* 3
- *1716 Nov 4* 33
- *1728 Sep 26* 34
- *1778 Jun 14* 27
- *1779 Dec 12* 12
- *1824 May 12* 5
- *1861 Jun 19* 39
- *1867 Jan 18* 20

Ellen Josephine
- *1887* 14

Emily Jane
- *1851 Aug 24* 6

Esther
- *1839* 14

Eva Adelaide
- *1878 Sep 28* 7

Evelyn Marion
- *1871 Dec 6* 9

Florence Edith
- *1890 Feb 2* 2

Hurst

Echlin Surname Ireland: 1600s to 1900s

Echlin Surname Ireland: 1600s to 1900s

Hurst

Hurst

About The Author

Donovan Hurst graduated from San Diego State University with a Bachelor of Arts in the major field of studies of History and a minor in the field of studies of Anthropology. He is a current member of The General Society of Mayflower Descendants and has been conducting genealogical research for over 10 years tracing back his ancestors to their ancestral homelands in Denmark, England, France, Germany, Ireland, Norway, and Scotland.

www.ingramcontent.com/pod-product-compliance
Lightning Source LLC
Chambersburg PA
CBHW081159270326
41930CB00014B/3225